AMANDA PAOLI

The Quick Negotiator: Mastering the Art of Fast and Effective Deal Making

A straight to the point book to get you negotiating faster and better.

First edition

This book was professionally typeset on Reedsy.
Find out more at reedsy.com

Contents

1 Introduction   1

2 Understanding the Foundations of Negotiation   3

3 Preparation: Gathering Information and Setting Objectives   11

4 Mastering Active Listening and Communication   16

5 Utilizing Empathy and Emotional Intelligence   22

6 Quick Persuasion Techniques   33

7 Creating Win-Win Solutions   38

8 Navigating Difficult Negotiation Situations   43

9 Mastering Quick Counteroffers and Compromises   49

10 Closing the Deal and Ensuring Long-Term Success   55

11 Post-Negotiation Strategies   59

12 Negotiating with Yourself   64

13 Conclusion   70

1

Introduction

Welcome! In this comprehensive guide, we will dive into the exciting world of negotiation and equip you with a diverse array of practical techniques for swift and successful negotiations. Whether you possess extensive experience in negotiations and wish to refine your skills or you are new to the world of deal-making and eager to navigate it successfully, this book provides invaluable insights to help you excel in different negotiation situations.

In today's fast-paced world, where time is a precious commodity, mastering the art of quick negotiation becomes more than just an advantage; it is a critical skill for staying ahead of the curve. Long, drawn-out negotiations can lead to missed opportunities, strained relationships, and unnecessary resource drain. By learning to negotiate swiftly and effectively, you will seize opportunities as they arise, navigate challenging situations adeptly, and build stronger connections with others, all while saving precious time.

This book is structured to provide you with a step-by-step journey through the essential principles of negotiation. We will start by exploring the psychology of human behavior in negotiations, enabling you to understand the motivations and desires that drive decision-making. Armed with this knowledge, we will then uncover a myriad of persuasion techniques that will enhance your ability to influence and create win-win outcomes.

Navigating challenging negotiation situations is an art in itself. You will learn how to handle aggressive or overly competitive negotiators, address resistance and stubbornness, and transform impasses into opportunities for growth and compromise. Armed with quick counteroffers and concession strategies, you will be able to make informed decisions under pressure, without sacrificing your interests and closing the deal. In the final chapters, we will guide you through the art of finalizing negotiations, formalizing agreements, and maintaining relationships after the deal is done. With "The Quick Negotiator" as your guide, you will be well-prepared to ensure long-term success and continued growth in your negotiation skills.

Throughout the book, we emphasize the ethical use of negotiation techniques, promoting respect, honesty, and integrity as the foundation for successful deal making. By incorporating these values into your negotiation approach, you will build trust and foster stronger relationships with your negotiating partners.

Embark on this transformative journey as you embrace the art of quick negotiation. As you progress through the pages, take the time to reflect on your past negotiation experiences and consider how the insights presented can be applied to future interactions. Practice the techniques, adapt them to your unique style, and observe the transformative impact they can have on your ability to negotiate with speed, precision, and finesse.

2

Understanding the Foundations of Negotiation

egotiation: The Art of the Deal

Negotiation is an age-old practice, deeply woven into the fabric of human interaction. It is the art of seeking agreement between two or more parties with different interests, needs, and objectives. From business transactions and legal settlements to personal relationships and everyday decisions, negotiation plays a pivotal role in shaping outcomes and relationships.

In this chapter, we will explore the foundational aspects of negotiation, helping you grasp the essence of this art and its significance in diverse contexts. Understanding the principles and dynamics of negotiation is essential as it forms the bedrock upon which all successful negotiation strategies are built.

Defining Negotiation

At its core, negotiation is a process where two or more parties come together to discuss and attempt to reach an agreement that satisfies their respective interests and objectives. Negotiation is not about dominating or overpowering the other party; it is about finding common ground, striking a balance, and arriving at a solution that benefits all involved.

Negotiation can take place in a multitude of settings, such as business negotiations, salary discussions, diplomatic treaties, interpersonal conflicts, or even something as simple as deciding where to eat with friends. The art of negotiation is ubiquitous and shapes our lives in ways both overt and subtle.

The Psychology of Negotiation

To become an adept negotiator, understanding human behavior and decision-making processes is paramount. People are influenced by various psychological factors, including emotions, biases, and cognitive limitations. Recognizing and accounting for these aspects can significantly impact the outcome of a negotiation. Throughout this book, we will delve into the psychology of negotiation, exploring how emotions, perception of fairness, and cognitive biases influence the decision-making process. Armed with this knowledge, you will be better equipped to navigate negotiations with sensitivity and precision, ultimately leading to better outcomes.

Different Negotiation Styles

Negotiators approach their craft with varying styles, each reflecting their personality, experiences, and cultural background. The three primary negotiation styles are competitive, cooperative, and collaborative.

1. Competitive negotiators are assertive and prioritize their interests

above all else. They are willing to use hardball tactics and may engage in aggressive behavior to achieve their objectives.

2. Cooperative negotiators seek mutual gain and aim to build positive, long-term relationships. They focus on collaboration and strive for win-win outcomes.

3. Collaborative negotiators embrace empathy and creativity, aiming to find solutions that benefit all parties. They prioritize joint problem-solving and seek to "expand the pie" rather than merely dividing it.

In this chapter, we will explore the advantages and disadvantages of each negotiation style, helping you identify your preferred approach and adapt it to various negotiation scenarios.

Overcoming Common Negotiation Roadblocks

Negotiations are seldom straightforward, and numerous challenges can impede progress. Common roadblocks include communication breakdowns, lack of trust, divergent interests, and an inability to understand the other party's perspective.

Understanding the foundations of negotiation is crucial to becoming a successful negotiator. As we progress through this book, you will gain valuable insights into the psychology of negotiation, different negotiation styles, and strategies for overcoming common roadblocks.

Negotiations can encounter various roadblocks that hinder the process and make it challenging to reach a mutually satisfactory agreement. Some common negotiation roadblocks include:

- **Lack of trust:** When there is a lack of trust between the parties, it can be difficult to believe the information shared or the commitments made, leading to suspicion and resistance.

- **Emotional reactions:** Emotions can run high during negotiations, leading to impulsive decision-making, heightened tensions, and an inability to focus on the core issues.

- **Communication barriers:** Ineffective communication, such as misunderstandings, misinterpretations, or language barriers, can prevent the parties from understanding each other's positions and interests accurately.

- **Fixed positions:** When both parties adopt rigid and unyielding positions, it becomes challenging to find common ground and explore flexible solutions.

- Competitive mindset: An overly competitive mindset, where parties are solely focused on "winning" at the expense of the other, can obstruct cooperation and compromise.

- **Lack of information:** Insufficient or incomplete information can lead to misunderstandings and an inability to make informed decisions.

- Time pressure: Negotiations conducted under tight deadlines may result in rushed decisions and compromises that do not fully address the parties' interests.

- **Power imbalances:** When there is a significant power disparity between the parties, the weaker party may feel compelled to agree to unfavorable terms, leading to an inequitable outcome.

- **Anchoring and framing effects:** The way information is presented or the first offer made can influence the negotiation's direction, leading to biased judgments and suboptimal outcomes.

- **Escalation of commitment:** A tendency to stick to initial positions even when it becomes evident that they are not working, leading to a prolonged stalemate.

- Group dynamics: Negotiating in a group setting can introduce complexities, as different individuals may have diverse perspectives and agendas.

- **Personal conflicts:** Past grievances or personal animosities can interfere with objective decision-making and lead to an emotionally charged negotiation environment.
- **Cultural differences:** Different cultural norms and communication styles can create misunderstandings and impede effective communication and collaboration.
- Incompatible interests: When parties' interests fundamentally clash, finding mutually acceptable solutions becomes more challenging.

To overcome these roadblocks, negotiators need to apply effective communication, empathy, problem-solving skills, and creativity. Building trust, actively listening, and focusing on underlying interests rather than fixed positions can help parties find common ground and navigate through roadblocks to reach successful negotiations. Additionally, maintaining a constructive and respectful approach can foster a cooperative negotiation atmosphere, even in the face of challenges.

To overcome negotiation roadblocks and improve the chances of reaching a successful outcome, consider the following strategies:

- **Build Trust:** Focus on building trust with the other party. Be honest, reliable, and transparent in your communication. Trust is essential for creating a positive negotiation environment where parties feel comfortable sharing information and making concessions.
- **Listen Actively:** Practice active listening to understand the other party's perspective fully. Listen not only to their words but also to their emotions and underlying interests. Demonstrate empathy

and show that you value their viewpoint.

- **Separate Emotions from the Issues:** Recognize and manage your own emotions and help the other party manage theirs. Avoid making emotional decisions and stay focused on the core issues and interests at hand.
- **Seek Common Ground:** Look for areas of agreement and shared interests. Highlight these commonalities to establish a foundation for cooperation and compromise.
- **Collaborate Instead of Compete:** Adopt a collaborative mindset instead of a competitive one. Focus on finding win-win solutions that address both parties' interests.
- **Generate Options:** Brainstorm a variety of potential solutions to the issues at hand. Be creative and explore different alternatives that could satisfy both parties' needs.
- **Use Objective Criteria:** Rely on objective criteria or standards to evaluate proposed solutions. This approach can help remove personal biases and facilitate a fair and logical decision-making process.
- **Stay Flexible:** Be open to making concessions and adjusting your position during the negotiation. Flexibility increases the likelihood of finding mutually beneficial agreements.
- **Educate Yourself:** Gather relevant information and data to support your arguments. Being well-informed strengthens your position and helps you make compelling arguments.
- **Establish a Positive Atmosphere:** Create a positive negotiation environment where both parties feel comfortable expressing their needs and concerns. Avoid adversarial behavior and focus on collaboration.
- **Manage Time Effectively:** Set realistic timelines for the negotiation and ensure that all parties have sufficient time to discuss their interests and options. Avoid rushing decisions under time pressure.

- **Address Power Imbalances:** If there is a significant power disparity between the parties, find ways to level the playing field and ensure the weaker party's interests are adequately considered.
- **Encourage Participation:** If negotiating in a group setting, ensure all team members have the opportunity to contribute and express their opinions.
- **Use Mediation or Third-Party Facilitation:** In cases where negotiations become deadlocked, consider involving a neutral mediator or facilitator to help bridge the gap and guide the negotiation process.

Remember that overcoming negotiation roadblocks requires patience, effective communication, and a willingness to find mutually acceptable solutions. Be prepared for challenges and be proactive in seeking ways to overcome them during the negotiation process.

Common Misconceptions and Fears

Many people approach negotiation with apprehension due to misconceptions about the process. Some may believe that negotiation is solely about manipulation, confrontation, or one party winning at the expense of the other. However, the truth is that successful negotiations are characterized by cooperation, understanding, and creative problem-solving, aiming for a win-win outcome where both parties benefit.

Others fear negotiation because they associate it with conflict or confrontation. While it's true that disagreements may arise during negotiations, skilled negotiators can turn these challenges into opportunities for collaboration and resolution.

The Benefits of Effective Negotiation: Effective negotiation offers a plethora of benefits, some of which include:

- **Maximizing Value:** Through negotiation, parties can identify and leverage shared interests, leading to creative solutions that maximize the overall value of the agreement.

- **Improved Relationships:** Skilled negotiators prioritize building rapport and trust, fostering positive long-term relationships with their counterparts.

- **Enhanced Problem-Solving Skills:** Negotiation sharpens analytical and critical thinking abilities, enabling negotiators to identify underlying issues and develop innovative solutions.

- **Increased Confidence:** The knowledge that one can effectively negotiate empowers individuals to approach challenges with confidence and determination.

- **Conflict Resolution:** Negotiation provides a structured framework for resolving conflicts peacefully and constructively.

- **Adaptability:** Negotiation equips individuals with the ability to adapt to changing circumstances and navigate unexpected challenges.

Negotiation is a potent tool that empowers individuals to achieve their goals, both professionally and personally. By embracing the true essence of negotiation, overcoming fears, and understanding its potential benefits, readers can embark on a journey to master the art of negotiation. Throughout this book, we will explore essential strategies, techniques, and principles that will empower you to become a proficient negotiator capable of achieving successful outcomes in any situation.

3

Preparation: Gathering Information and Setting Objectives

The success of any negotiation hinges on the level of preparation undertaken before entering the negotiating room. In this chapter, we will delve into the crucial process of preparation, equipping you with the tools and strategies needed to lay a strong foundation for your negotiations.

The Importance of Thorough Preparation

Effective negotiation preparation is the key differentiator between a successful negotiator and an average one. It allows you to enter negotiations with clarity, confidence, and a deep understanding of the issues at hand. Adequate preparation minimizes surprises, reduces anxiety, and maximizes your ability to achieve your objectives.

We will explore the fundamental elements of preparation, including defining your goals, gathering relevant information, and anticipating potential challenges. By investing time and effort in preparation, you can significantly increase your chances of securing favorable outcomes.

Identifying Your Objectives and Priorities

Before entering any negotiation, it is essential to have a clear understanding of what you hope to achieve. Identifying your objectives and priorities will serve as your guiding compass throughout the negotiation process. Ask yourself:

- What are your must-have outcomes, and what are your nice-to-have outcomes?
- What is the ideal result you would like to achieve, and what is the least you are willing to accept?
- Are there any specific constraints or red lines you must adhere to?

By establishing your objectives and priorities, you will be better equipped to maintain focus during the negotiation and avoid being swayed by distractions or emotional impulses.

Researching the Other Party's Interests and Goals

Understanding the interests and goals of the other party is equally crucial to successful negotiation. Conduct thorough research on their needs, motivations, and constraints. By gaining insight into their perspective, you can tailor your approach and communication to resonate with their interests.

Research can involve gathering information through various channels, such as conducting interviews, studying industry trends, analyzing past negotiations, and leveraging available data. Armed with this knowledge, you will be better prepared to identify potential areas of alignment and craft persuasive arguments that resonate with the other party.

Anticipating Potential Objections and Preparing Responses

In any negotiation, there will likely be objections and challenges that arise. Anticipating these potential roadblocks enables you to devise strategic responses in advance. Consider the objections that the other party may raise and brainstorm possible counterarguments. Preparation will empower you to address objections confidently and mitigate potential conflicts during the negotiation. By proactively addressing concerns, you demonstrate your thoroughness and commitment to finding solutions, thus fostering a more cooperative negotiating environment.

Anticipating potential objections and preparing responses in negotiations is a crucial aspect of being well-prepared and persuasive during the negotiation process. Here's how to effectively anticipate objections and develop responses:

- **Know your audience:** Understand the other party's perspective, needs, and concerns. This knowledge allows you to anticipate objections they may raise based on their interests and goals.
- **Identify common objections:** Based on your experience with similar negotiations, identify common objections that might arise. Consider past interactions or industry standards to anticipate recurring objections.
- **Listen actively:** During the negotiation, actively listen to the other party's statements and questions. Pay attention to signals that indicate potential objections.
- **Put yourself in their shoes:** Empathize with the other party's position and think about the objections they may raise from their point of view.
- **Address objections proactively:** If you anticipate certain ob-

jections, incorporate your responses into your initial proposal or presentation. Address these concerns before they are raised.

- **Prepare evidence and data:** Back up your position with relevant evidence, data, and examples. Having strong supporting material can bolster your arguments and make your responses more compelling.
- **Use objective criteria:** When responding to objections, refer to objective criteria or industry standards. This approach can add credibility to your responses.
- **Stay composed:** Respond to objections calmly and professionally. Avoid becoming defensive or emotional, as it can weaken your position.
- Highlight benefits and value: Emphasize the benefits and value of your proposal. Explain how your proposition meets the other party's needs and objectives.
- **Offer alternatives:** If the other party raises objections, be prepared to offer alternative solutions that address their concerns while still aligning with your interests.
- **Bridge to common ground:** Find areas of agreement and build on those to bridge any gaps created by objections. Demonstrating a willingness to work together can create a more cooperative negotiation environment.
- **Re frame objections positively:** Instead of simply refuting objections, reframe them in a positive light. Show how the perceived challenges can lead to opportunities or benefits.
- **Maintain flexibility:** Be willing to adjust your position if the other party raises valid objections. Negotiation often involves give-and-take, and being open to compromise can lead to mutually beneficial outcomes.
- **Practice responses:** Role-play potential objections with a colleague or advisor to refine your responses and improve your ability

to handle objections effectively.

By anticipating potential objections and preparing thoughtful responses, you can enhance your negotiation skills and increase the likelihood of achieving successful outcomes that satisfy both parties.

Ethics and Integrity in Negotiation Preparation

While robust preparation is crucial for successful negotiations, it is essential to maintain ethical standards throughout the process. Avoid resorting to deceptive tactics or misrepresenting information, as such practices can damage trust and compromise the integrity of the negotiation.

Negotiation is not a zero-sum game; rather, it is an opportunity for collaboration and creative problem-solving. By approaching preparation with integrity and respect for the other party, you can lay the groundwork for a constructive negotiation that yields lasting, mutually beneficial results.

4

Mastering Active Listening and Communication

I n the realm of negotiation, effective communication is the bedrock upon which successful deals are built. However, communication is not just about speaking; it is about listening actively and understanding the needs and desires of the other party. In this chapter, we will explore the art of active listening and communication, equipping you with the essential tools to foster rapport and build trust during negotiations.

The Power of Active Listening

Active listening is the cornerstone of effective communication. It involves fully concentrating, understanding, responding, and remembering what the other party is saying. By engaging in active listening, you demonstrate respect for the other party's perspective, creating an environment conducive to open and honest dialogue.

Practicing active listening goes beyond merely hearing the words spoken; it involves empathizing with the emotions and intentions behind those words. As you master the art of active listening, you will be better equipped to pick up on underlying interests, concerns, and motivations, enabling you to tailor your negotiation strategy accordingly.

Verbal and Non-Verbal Communication Techniques

Communication encompasses both verbal and non-verbal cues. While the spoken words convey the content of your message, non-verbal cues, such as body language and tone of voice, convey emotions and attitudes. Maintaining consistency between verbal and non-verbal cues is essential for building credibility and trust during negotiations.

Verbal communication techniques, such as choosing clear and concise language, framing statements positively, and asking open-ended questions to encourage the other party to share more information is necessary in advancing to your desired outcome.

Using effective one-liners in negotiations can be a powerful way to convey your points succinctly and assertively. Here are some negotiation one-liners you can use:

- "Let's find a win-win solution that benefits both of us."
- "I appreciate your offer, but I was hoping for something closer to [your desired outcome]."
- "If we can agree on [specific point], I believe we can move forward successfully."
- "I understand your position, and I need you to understand mine."
- "Could you help me understand the reasoning behind your proposal?"
- "Let's explore other options that align with both our interests."

- "Can we meet in the middle to reach a fair agreement?"
- "Time is of the essence; can we work on finalizing this by [specific date]?"
- "I'd be more comfortable with this if we could add [specific condition]."
- "What can we do to make this deal more appealing to both parties?"

Remember, the key to successful negotiation is not just using one-liners but also active listening, understanding the other party's needs, and being open to compromise. Use these one-liners as tools to steer the conversation toward a mutually beneficial outcome.

Building Rapport and Trust

Rapport and trust are the cornerstones of successful negotiations. Building rapport involves establishing a positive and harmonious connection with the other party, fostering a sense of mutual understanding and respect. Trust, on the other hand, is the belief that both parties will honor their commitments and act in good faith throughout the negotiation process.

Building trust and rapport in negotiations is crucial to creating a positive and productive atmosphere where both parties feel comfortable discussing their interests and concerns. Here are some strategies to help you build trust and rapport during negotiations:

- **Active Listening:** Listen attentively to the other party's concerns and viewpoints. Show genuine interest in what they have to say and avoid interrupting or rushing to respond. Paraphrase their statements to demonstrate that you understand their perspective.
- **Empathy and Understanding:** Put yourself in the other party's

shoes and try to understand their needs, motivations, and constraints. Showing empathy helps create a sense of connection and mutual respect.

- **Transparency and Honesty:** Be open and honest about your interests and constraints. Avoid withholding important information or making false promises, as this can damage trust and credibility.
- **Consistency:** Be consistent in your messaging and actions throughout the negotiation process. Trust is built when parties can rely on each other's words and commitments.
- **Focus on Common Interests:** Identify shared interests and goals between the parties. Emphasize how the negotiation can lead to mutual benefits and positive outcomes.
- **Avoid Personal Attacks:** Keep the negotiation focused on the issues and avoid personal attacks or aggressive behavior. Treat the other party with respect, even when disagreements arise.
- **Negotiate in Good Faith:** Demonstrate a genuine willingness to reach a fair and reasonable agreement. Avoid using manipulative tactics or taking extreme positions solely for strategic purposes.
- **Follow Through on Agreements:** If an agreement is reached, ensure that you fulfill your commitments promptly and as promised. This reinforces trust and shows that you are a reliable negotiation partner.
- **Be Patient:** Building trust takes time, so be patient and persistent in your efforts to establish a positive relationship with the other party.
- **Find Common Ground Outside the Negotiation:** If possible, engage in activities or discussions outside of the negotiation context to establish a more personal connection. This can help build rapport and trust.

Remember that trust and rapport are not one-time achievements but ongoing efforts throughout the negotiation process. Building a strong foundation of trust can lead to more successful and sustainable agreements for both parties involved.

Overcoming Communication Barriers and Misunderstandings

Communication barriers can impede productive negotiations. These barriers may include language differences, cultural nuances, personal biases, or misinterpretation of messages. Recognizing and overcoming these barriers is essential for ensuring clear and effective communication.

Overcoming communication barriers and misunderstandings in negotiations is essential for achieving successful outcomes. Here are some strategies to help you navigate these challenges effectively:

- **Active Listening:** Pay close attention to what the other party is saying, and ask clarifying questions to ensure you understand their perspective fully. Paraphrase their statements to confirm your understanding.
- **Encourage Open Communication:** Create a supportive environment where all parties feel comfortable expressing their thoughts and concerns openly. Encourage them to share their viewpoints without fear of judgment.
- **Use Clear and Simple Language:** Avoid jargon or complex language that could be misinterpreted. Use clear and straightforward language to convey your ideas and intentions.
- **Seek Feedback:** Ask for feedback from the other party on your communication style and whether they feel their concerns are being understood. This can help identify any potential misunderstandings.

- **Watch Non-Verbal Cues:** Pay attention to body language and facial expressions, as they can provide valuable insights into the other party's feelings and intentions.

- **Address Cultural Differences:** Be aware of cultural nuances that may affect communication styles and interpretations. Be respectful and sensitive to cultural diversity.

- **Manage Emotions:** Emotions can escalate misunderstandings. Stay calm and composed, and encourage a rational and respectful exchange of ideas.

- **Ask for Examples:** If something is unclear, ask the other party to provide examples or scenarios to illustrate their point further.

- **Use Visual Aids:** If appropriate, use visual aids like charts or diagrams to explain complex ideas. Visual aids can enhance understanding and provide a common reference point.

- **Summarize and Recap:** Periodically summarize the main points of the discussion to ensure both parties are on the same page. Recap important agreements or decisions to avoid any misinterpretations.

- **Bring in a Mediator:** If communication barriers persist, consider involving a neutral third party to mediate the negotiation. A mediator can help facilitate communication and find common ground.

- **Be Patient and Persistent:** Overcoming communication barriers may take time. Be patient, and continue to invest effort in improving communication throughout the negotiation process.

Remember that effective communication is a two-way process. Both parties must be committed to understanding each other's perspectives and working together to find mutually beneficial solutions. By actively addressing communication barriers and misunderstandings, you can enhance the likelihood of reaching a successful negotiation outcome.

5

Utilizing Empathy and Emotional Intelligence

I n the high-stakes world of negotiation, emotions often run high, and the ability to understand and manage these emotions can make the difference between a successful outcome and a missed opportunity. We will explore the critical role of empathy and emotional intelligence in negotiation, empowering you to navigate emotions effectively and create win-win solutions.

The Power of Empathy in Negotiations

Empathy is the capacity to understand and share the feelings, perspectives, and needs of others. In negotiation, demonstrating empathy helps build trust and rapport, as it shows the other party that you genuinely care about their concerns and interests. Practicing empathy requires active engagement with the other party's emotions and viewpoints. By putting yourself in their shoes and considering their unique circumstances, you gain valuable insights into their underlying needs and motivations. Empathy fosters a collaborative negotiating environment, increasing the likelihood of finding solutions that satisfy both parties.

The power of empathy in negotiation cannot be overstated. Demonstrating empathy allows negotiators to understand and connect with the other party on a deeper level, which can lead to more successful and mutually beneficial outcomes. Here are some examples of how empathy can be powerful in negotiations:

- **Understanding Needs and Motivations:** A salesperson trying to close a deal with a potential client demonstrates empathy by listening attentively to the client's needs and motivations. By understanding the client's pain points and desired outcomes, the salesperson can tailor their proposal to address those specific concerns, increasing the chances of a successful agreement.

- **Building Trust:** A labor union negotiator shows empathy toward the management team during contract negotiations. By acknowledging the challenges faced by the company and genuinely considering their constraints, the union negotiator fosters an environment of trust and cooperation. This can lead to more constructive discussions and a higher likelihood of reaching a fair agreement for both parties.

- **Resolving Conflicts:** Two business partners have a disagreement about the direction of the company. Instead of becoming entrenched in their positions, they both take the time to understand each other's perspectives and the underlying motivations driving their stances. Through empathy, they find common ground and are better equipped to find a compromise that aligns with both of their visions for the company's future.

- **Handling Difficult Negotiations:** In a complex and high-stakes negotiation, a diplomat practices empathy by considering the cultural sensitivities and historical context of the other party. By showing understanding and respect for their concerns, the diplomat fosters an atmosphere of goodwill and reduces the likelihood of unnecessary conflict.

- **Maintaining Long-Term Relationships:** An ongoing negotiation between a supplier and a buyer could be fraught with tension due to pricing disagreements. However, both parties understand the importance of their relationship and the value they bring to each other's businesses. Through empathy, they find ways to address pricing issues while preserving their long-term collaboration.

- **Winning Over Opponents:** In a political negotiation, a candidate seeking support from a rival faction demonstrates empathy by actively listening to their concerns and incorporating some of their ideas into their platform. This gesture builds bridges and may win over some of the opponent's supporters.

- **De-escalating Tense Situations:** In a labor negotiation that is at risk of becoming confrontational, both sides practice empathy by acknowledging the emotions and frustrations of the other party. By recognizing the human aspect of the situation, they create a space for more constructive dialogue and a better chance of finding common ground.

Empathy helps negotiators view the negotiation from the perspective of the other party, fostering a deeper understanding of their interests, values, and emotions. This understanding can lead to more creative solutions and build stronger relationships, making empathy a powerful tool in negotiation strategies.

Leveraging Emotional Intelligence

Emotional intelligence is the ability to recognize and manage both your emotions and the emotions of others. Negotiators with high emotional intelligence are better equipped to navigate the emotional ups and downs of the negotiation process, leading to more constructive and productive interactions.

Leveraging emotional intelligence in negotiations can significantly enhance your ability to understand, connect with, and influence others effectively. Emotional intelligence involves being aware of your emotions and those of others, and using that awareness to manage relationships and navigate social situations successfully. Here are some tips on how to apply emotional intelligence in negotiations:

- **Self-awareness:** Recognize and understand your own emotions during the negotiation process. Be aware of how they might affect your decision-making and communication. If you notice yourself becoming angry, anxious, or overly emotional, take a moment to step back and regain your composure before continuing the negotiation.
- **Empathy:** Practice empathizing with the other party's emotions and perspectives. Try to understand their needs, desires, and concerns. Active listening is crucial here, as it helps you pick up on nonverbal cues and truly comprehend their underlying emotions and motivations.
- **Manage emotions:** Emotions can run high during negotiations, and that's normal. However, it's essential to manage your emotions constructively. Avoid reacting impulsively or aggressively. Instead, find ways to express yourself calmly and assertively.
- **Build rapport:** Create a positive and supportive atmosphere during negotiations. Establishing rapport can foster trust and openness, making it easier for both parties to work together towards a mutually beneficial agreement.
- Recognize emotions in others: Pay close attention to the emotions displayed by the other party. Look for signs of frustration, excitement, hesitation, or satisfaction. Understanding their emotions

can give you valuable insights into their underlying interests and priorities.

- **Adapt your communication:** Tailor your communication style to connect with the emotions of the other party. For example, if they seem anxious, use reassuring language. If they appear enthusiastic, acknowledge and encourage their positive feelings.
- **Stay patient:** Negotiations can be challenging and time-consuming. Emotional intelligence allows you to remain patient, even in the face of obstacles or difficult emotions. Patience helps you avoid making hasty decisions that may not be in your best interest.
- **Problem-solving orientation:** Focus on the underlying interests and needs of both parties rather than just getting what you want. Emotional intelligence helps you identify creative solutions that address everyone's concerns.
- **Negotiate with win-win in mind:** Seek mutually beneficial outcomes rather than trying to "win" at the expense of the other party. Emotional intelligence enables you to create an environment where both sides feel like they've achieved a fair deal.
- **Resolve conflicts diplomatically:** If conflicts arise during negotiations, use emotional intelligence to de-escalate the situation and find common ground. Avoid attacking the other party personally and instead address the issues constructively.

Incorporating emotional intelligence into your negotiation approach can lead to more successful and satisfying outcomes. By understanding and managing emotions effectively, you can build stronger relationships, foster cooperation, and achieve mutually beneficial results.

Recognizing and Managing Emotions During Negotiations

In the heat of negotiations, emotions can run the gamut from excitement to frustration and from joy to disappointment. It is essential to recognize and manage these emotions to maintain a balanced and composed demeanor throughout the negotiation.

Here are some practical tips to help you recognize and manage emotions effectively:

- **Practice self-awareness:** Be mindful of your own emotions throughout the negotiation. Pay attention to how you feel and how your emotions may influence your decisions and behavior. If you notice strong emotions arising, take a moment to acknowledge them without judgment.
- **Identify triggers:** Be aware of situations or topics that tend to evoke strong emotional reactions in you. Knowing your triggers can help you anticipate and prepare for potential emotional challenges during the negotiation.
- **Take breaks when needed:** If you find yourself overwhelmed by emotions during the negotiation, don't hesitate to request a short break. Stepping away from the discussion can provide you with the opportunity to regain your composure and think more clearly.
- **Practice active listening:** Pay close attention to the emotions expressed by the other party through their words, tone of voice, and body language. Active listening allows you to understand their feelings and motivations better.
- **Use empathy:** Put yourself in the other party's shoes and try to understand their perspective and emotions. Empathy can help you build rapport and foster a more cooperative negotiation environment.
- **Control your body language:** Be mindful of your own body language, as it can convey your emotions even if you're trying to hide them. Maintain open and positive body language to create a

comfortable atmosphere for communication.

- **Pause before reacting:** If the other party says something that triggers an emotional response, take a moment before responding. This pause allows you to collect your thoughts and respond rationally instead of reacting impulsively.

- **Practice emotional regulation techniques:** Develop strategies to manage your emotions during negotiations. These techniques may include deep breathing, visualization, or mentally reframing the situation in a more positive light.

- **Address emotions directly:** If you sense that emotions are affecting the negotiation process, address them directly. Acknowledge the emotions in a respectful manner and consider how they might be influencing the discussion.

- **Stay focused on the negotiation goals:** Remind yourself of the objectives you want to achieve through the negotiation. Keeping your goals in mind can help you maintain focus and perspective even when emotions run high.

- **Seek support:** If possible, have a trusted colleague or advisor present during the negotiation. They can provide valuable feedback, help you recognize emotional responses, and offer suggestions to manage emotions effectively.

Remember, emotions are a natural part of the negotiation process, and it's essential to acknowledge and manage them skillfully. By recognizing and controlling your emotions, as well as understanding and empathizing with the emotions of the other party, you can create a more constructive and productive negotiation experience for everyone involved.

Using Emotional Triggers Strategically

While emotions should not drive the negotiation entirely, judiciously leveraging emotional triggers can be a powerful tool to influence decisions. Understanding the emotional hot buttons of the other party allows you to tailor your messaging and proposals in ways that resonate deeply with them. However, it is crucial to use emotional triggers responsibly and ethically. Avoid manipulative tactics that may damage trust or compromise the integrity of the negotiation. Instead, focus on using emotional triggers to highlight the positive outcomes and value of the proposed solutions.

Emotional triggers can significantly impact negotiations, either positively or negatively. Strategically managing emotional triggers can help you maintain control, build rapport, and steer the negotiation process towards a favorable outcome. Here are some tips on how to handle emotional triggers strategically during negotiations:

- **Be aware of emotional triggers:** Recognize common emotional triggers that might arise during negotiations. These triggers can include topics related to money, trust, personal values, deadlines, or past conflicts. Anticipating potential triggers allows you to prepare and plan your responses in advance.
- **Stay calm and composed:** Emotional triggers can cause tensions to escalate. As a strategic negotiator, aim to remain calm and composed, especially when faced with provocative statements or behavior. Your ability to control your emotions can influence the other party to follow suit.
- **Empathize and acknowledge emotions:** When emotional triggers surface, demonstrate empathy and acknowledge the other party's feelings. Validate their emotions without necessarily agreeing with their perspective. This approach can de-escalate tensions and create a more constructive negotiation environment.

- **Use active listening:** Listen actively to the concerns and frustrations expressed by the other party. Give them the space to share their emotions, and show that you genuinely understand their point of view. This approach can help defuse emotional tensions and make the other party feel heard and respected.
- **Redirect the focus:** If emotional triggers threaten to derail the negotiation, strategically shift the focus back to the main issues at hand. Gently remind both parties of the common goals and objectives, refocusing the discussion on finding solutions.
- **Reframe negative emotions:** Help the other party reframe negative emotions in a more positive light. For example, if they express frustration, highlight the progress made in the negotiation or the potential for finding common ground.
- **Avoid personal attacks:** Stay focused on the issues and avoid making personal attacks or becoming defensive when emotional triggers are pulled. Keep the negotiation professional and centered on the interests of both parties.
- **Create a positive atmosphere:** Use positive language and gestures to foster a more cooperative negotiation atmosphere. Compliment the other party's efforts, highlight areas of agreement, and show appreciation for their input.
- **Use humor when appropriate:** Humor can diffuse tension and help to build rapport between negotiators. Use it judiciously and in a lighthearted manner to ease emotional tension during the negotiation process.
- **Take strategic breaks:** If emotions become overwhelming, consider taking a short break. Use this time to collect your thoughts, regain composure, and refocus on the negotiation's objectives.
- **Establish a code of conduct:** Before starting negotiations, agree on a code of conduct that outlines appropriate behavior and communication. This agreement can serve as a reference point

if emotional triggers arise, reminding all parties to stay respectful and constructive.

Incorporating these strategies to handle emotional triggers can positively influence the negotiation process and enhance the likelihood of achieving a mutually beneficial agreement. Remember that emotional intelligence and strategic thinking play essential roles in managing emotions effectively during negotiations.

Balancing Empathy with Assertiveness

In negotiations, striking a balance between empathy and assertiveness is critical. While empathy fosters collaboration and understanding, assertiveness ensures that your interests and needs are adequately represented.

Here are key points on how to balance empathy with assertiveness in negotiations:

- **Validating Emotions with Assertive Positioning:** While acknowledging the other party's emotions, express your own position assertively. For instance, you can say, "I hear your concerns, and I want to find a solution that works for both of us. Here's what I propose..."
- **Building Rapport with Clear Communication:** Use empathetic communication to build rapport. Share your own experiences or challenges to demonstrate that you understand the human side of the negotiation. However, balance this with clear and direct communication of your objectives and requirements.
- **Understanding Interests with Problem-Solving:** Seek to understand the underlying interests and needs of both parties through

empathetic questioning. Then, assertively propose potential solutions that address those interests effectively.

- **Compromise with Mutual Gain in Mind:** Be open to compromising on certain aspects while ensuring that the final agreement meets the core interests of both parties. This approach shows empathy for the other party's concerns while assertively protecting your essential needs.
- **Recognizing Emotions without Yielding to Pressure:** If the other party becomes emotional, acknowledge their feelings without letting it pressure you into accepting unfavorable terms. Maintain assertiveness while staying respectful and composed.
- **Negotiating Deadlines with Flexibility:** If the negotiation involves time constraints, empathize with the other party's time pressures. Then, assertively propose a flexible timeline that allows for thorough consideration of the agreement's terms.
- **Navigating Cultural Differences with Sensitivity:** Be sensitive to cultural differences that may impact communication styles and expressions of emotions. Demonstrate empathy by adapting your approach, while still clearly conveying your position.
- **Responding to Criticism with Diplomacy:** If faced with criticism or negative feedback, empathize with the other party's concerns and then assertively address any misconceptions or provide clarifications.
- **Expressing Disagreements with Respect:** In case of disagreements, use assertive language to articulate your point of view while showing respect for the other party's perspective.

Balancing empathy with assertiveness requires adaptability and emotional intelligence. It allows negotiators to connect with the other party on a human level while maintaining clarity and focus on achieving their negotiation objectives.

6

Quick Persuasion Techniques

I n the world of negotiation, persuasion is a powerful tool that can tip the scales in your favor. In this chapter, we will explore quick persuasion techniques that leverage human psychology to influence decisions and create win-win outcomes.

The Principle of Reciprocity

Reciprocity is the social norm that encourages people to return favors and kindness they receive. In negotiation, offering concessions or demonstrating goodwill can trigger the reciprocity principle, encouraging the other party to reciprocate in kind.

We will delve into the art of using reciprocity strategically, ensuring that your concessions are purposeful and create a sense of obligation in the other party. By employing reciprocity effectively, you can foster a cooperative negotiating environment and set the stage for mutual give-and-take.

The Power of Social Proof and Authority

Social proof and authority are psychological factors that influence decision-making. Social proof is the tendency to follow the actions of others when uncertain, while authority is the inclination to comply with figures perceived as knowledgeable or influential. By highlighting relevant success stories, testimonials, or case studies, you can appeal to the principle of social proof, providing evidence that others have found value in your proposals. Additionally, positioning yourself or your organization as authoritative figures in the field can bolster your credibility and influence.

Utilizing Scarcity and Urgency

Scarcity and urgency create a sense of value and scarcity, compelling people to act promptly to secure an opportunity. By strategically incorporating scarcity and urgency into your negotiation proposals, you can drive a swift decision-making process and incentivize the other party to seize the opportunity before it vanishes. However, it is essential to use scarcity and urgency ethically, ensuring that the scarcity is genuine and the urgency is not manufactured. Misleading tactics can backfire and damage the trust built during the negotiation.

Utilizing scarcity and urgency can be effective negotiation tactics when used ethically and appropriately. These tactics leverage the psychological principles of fear of loss and time pressure to encourage the other party to act quickly or agree to your terms. Here's how to use scarcity and urgency in negotiations:

- **Scarcity:** Emphasize the limited availability of a product, service, or opportunity to create a sense of urgency. For example, mention that there are only a few units left in stock or that the offer is available for a limited time.

- **Urgency:** Create a time-sensitive atmosphere by setting clear deadlines for the negotiation process or the acceptance of an offer. Time pressure can motivate the other party to make a decision promptly.
- **Highlight Unique Benefits:** Emphasize the unique benefits of your proposal that make it stand out from other options available to the other party. By showcasing the scarcity of these advantages, you increase their perceived value.
- **Provide Social Proof:** Demonstrate that others have taken advantage of the same opportunity or offer, creating a sense of urgency to avoid missing out on a beneficial deal.
- **Use Real Data:** Support your claims of scarcity or urgency with actual data, such as sales figures, customer reviews, or market trends, to enhance credibility and legitimacy.
- **Offer Incentives:** To encourage prompt action, consider providing incentives for early agreement or quick decision-making, such as discounts or additional benefits.
- **Maintain Ethical Boundaries:** While using scarcity and urgency can be effective, be honest and transparent about the actual availability or time constraints. Avoid creating artificial scarcity or imposing false deadlines.
- **Stay Flexible:** Allow some room for negotiation despite the scarcity or urgency to avoid coming across as inflexible or manipulative.
- **Use Discretion:** Be mindful of the other party's situation and avoid exerting excessive pressure that could strain the relationship or lead to undesirable outcomes.
- **Know When to Employ:** Not all negotiations require the use of scarcity and urgency. Assess the situation and the other party's motivations before deciding to implement these tactics.

Remember, while scarcity and urgency can be persuasive tools, overusing them or applying them unethically may damage trust and compromise the negotiation process. It is crucial to strike a balance and use these tactics responsibly to create a win-win outcome for both parties.

Effective Storytelling in Negotiation

Storytelling is a compelling tool to influence and persuade. Human brains are wired to remember stories better than abstract information. By weaving a narrative around your proposals, you can engage the other party emotionally and make your arguments more memorable and relatable.

- **Make it Personal:** Share relevant personal experiences or anecdotes to humanize your perspective and build trust.
- **Create a Common Ground:** Find shared experiences or values in your stories to foster understanding and collaboration.
- **Address Concerns:** Use storytelling to clarify your intentions and dispel misconceptions about your position.
- **Appeal to Emotions:** Craft compelling stories that evoke emotions and make your points more persuasive.
- **Keep it Relevant:** Ensure your storytelling stays focused on the negotiation topic and its relevance.
- **Use Visual Language:** Paint vivid pictures with words to enhance the impact of your stories.
- **Highlight Success Stories:** Share real-life examples of successful outcomes from your proposed solutions.
- **Be Authentic:** Be genuine and sincere in your storytelling to build rapport with the other party.
- **Listen to Their Stories:** Be open to hearing the other party's stories to better understand their perspective.

- **Practice Empathy:** Use stories to demonstrate empathy and willingness to work towards mutually beneficial solutions.

Remember that storytelling should complement your negotiation strategy, not replace it. Combine effective communication, active listening, and other negotiation techniques with storytelling to enhance your chances of reaching a successful outcome.

7

Creating Win-Win Solutions

I n negotiation, the most satisfying outcomes are those where all parties walk away feeling like winners. Creating win-win solutions involves a collaborative approach that maximizes gains for both parties and fosters long-term relationships.

Understanding the Concept of "Expanding the Pie"

The traditional notion of negotiation revolves around dividing the pie, where one party's gain is perceived as another's loss. In contrast, expanding the pie focuses on increasing the value of the resources being negotiated, allowing for more significant gains for all parties involved. By embracing the concept of expanding the pie, you can shift the negotiation from a zero-sum game to a cooperative endeavor, where creativity and collaboration lead to outcomes that exceed initial expectations.

Techniques for Finding Mutually Beneficial Solutions

Finding win-win solutions requires a creative and open-minded approach to problem-solving. We will explore techniques such as brainstorming, exploring alternative options, and re framing problems to uncover mutually beneficial solutions.

Finding mutually beneficial solutions is the cornerstone of successful negotiations. These techniques help negotiators identify common ground and create agreements that satisfy the interests of all parties involved. Here are some effective techniques for finding mutually beneficial solutions:

- **Interest-Based Negotiation:** Focus on the underlying interests and needs of both parties rather than rigid positions. Ask open-ended questions to understand their motivations and concerns better.
- **Brainstorming:** Encourage creative thinking and generate a variety of potential solutions. The goal is to explore different possibilities that address each party's interests.
- **Value Creation:** Seek opportunities to expand the pie by identifying additional resources or elements that can enhance the overall value of the agreement.
- **Trade-offs and Concessions:** Look for areas where you can make concessions without compromising your core interests. In exchange, request concessions from the other party on issues more critical to you.
- **Win-Win Mindset:** Embrace a collaborative mindset, where both parties aim for mutually beneficial outcomes. Avoid win-lose approaches that may harm the relationship and long-term prospects.
- **Objective Criteria:** Rely on objective standards or benchmarks to evaluate proposed solutions. This approach removes subjectivity and provides a basis for fair and reasonable agreements.

- **Explore Multiple Agreements:** Consider different combinations of terms and conditions to find the most favorable arrangement for both sides.
- **Long-Term Perspective:** Evaluate the potential long-term consequences of the agreement. A sustainable relationship can lead to more opportunities and benefits in the future.
- **Utilize Third-Party Facilitators:** In complex negotiations, consider involving neutral third parties or mediators to assist in finding mutually beneficial solutions.
- **Contingency Planning:** Include contingency clauses in the agreement to account for unexpected events or changes in circumstances. This flexibility can maintain fairness and adaptability over time.
- **Shared Goals and Values:** Emphasize shared goals and values between the parties to strengthen the sense of partnership and collaboration.
- **Active Listening and Empathy:** Listen attentively to the other party's concerns and demonstrate empathy for their needs. This approach builds trust and encourages open communication.
- **Consistent Communication:** Maintain clear and consistent communication throughout the negotiation process. This helps in avoiding misunderstandings and building rapport.
- **Building Relationships:** Invest in building a positive and constructive relationship with the other party. A strong relationship can foster cooperation and lead to more beneficial agreements.

By employing these techniques, negotiators can create win-win outcomes that satisfy the interests of both parties and pave the way for successful and enduring agreements.

Negotiating with Multiple Parties

Negotiating with multiple parties, also known as multiparty negotiation, can be complex and challenging. It involves managing various interests, dynamics, and relationships among the parties involved. Here are some strategies to effectively navigate negotiations with multiple parties:

1. **Preparation is Key:** Before entering the negotiation, thoroughly research and understand the interests, priorities, and positions of each party. Identify potential areas of agreement and potential areas of conflict.

2. **Establish Clear Objectives:** Define your objectives and what you hope to achieve from the negotiation. Understand the common goals that can be pursued collectively and those that may be unique to each party.

3. **Build Relationships:** Cultivate positive relationships with all parties involved. Establishing trust and rapport can lead to smoother negotiations and increased cooperation.

4. **Identify Common Ground:** Look for shared interests and goals among the parties. Emphasize and build upon these commonalities to foster collaboration.

5. **Manage Communication:** Communication is vital in multiparty negotiations. Ensure that all parties have an equal opportunity to express their perspectives and concerns. Facilitate open dialogue and active listening.

6. **Use a Neutral Facilitator:** In complex negotiations, it may be beneficial to have a neutral third party act as a facilitator or mediator. This person can help manage conflicts, keep discussions on track, and ensure fairness.

7. **Address Individual Concerns:** Recognize and address the unique concerns of each party involved. Tailor your proposals to accommodate their specific needs while still aiming for a mutually acceptable solution.

41

8. **Brainstorm Creative Solutions:** Encourage all parties to contribute ideas and explore creative solutions that satisfy multiple interests. Avoid rigid positions and be open to compromise.

9. **Handle Conflicts Constructively:** Conflicts may arise between different parties. When they do, address them constructively and find ways to de-escalate tensions. Avoid personal attacks and focus on the issues at hand.

10. **Create a Win-Win Outcome:** Aim for a win-win outcome where all parties feel their interests are respected and satisfied. This approach fosters long-term relationships and sets the stage for future cooperation.

11. **Document Agreements:** When consensus is reached, document the agreed-upon terms in writing to avoid misunderstandings or disputes later on.

12. **Be Patient and Persistent:** Multiparty negotiations can be time-consuming. Be patient and persistent throughout the process. Avoid rushing to reach an agreement at the expense of a fair and comprehensive resolution.

Remember that multiparty negotiations can be intricate and may require flexibility and adaptability. By maintaining a collaborative and open approach, you increase the chances of achieving a successful outcome that benefits all parties involved.

Maintaining a Positive and Collaborative Attitude

A positive and collaborative attitude is contagious and sets the tone for productive negotiations. By maintaining a solution-oriented mindset and demonstrating flexibility when necessary, you can foster an environment that encourages creativity and cooperation.

8

Navigating Difficult Negotiation Situations

In the unpredictable landscape of negotiation, challenging situations are bound to arise. In this chapter, we will explore strategies for navigating difficult negotiation scenarios, empowering you to handle aggressive counterparts, address resistance, and turn deadlocks into opportunities for growth.

Handling Aggressive or Overly Competitive and Stubborn Negotiators

Dealing with aggressive negotiators requires a delicate balance of assertiveness and composure. We will discuss techniques for responding to aggression without escalating the situation, maintaining your ground, and redirecting the conversation towards constructive dialogue.

Handling aggressive or overly competitive negotiators can be challenging, but it's essential to remain composed and strategic in your approach. Here are some effective ways to manage such situations:

- **Stay Calm and Assertive:** Maintain your composure and respond to aggressive behavior with assertiveness. Avoid getting drawn into a confrontational exchange, as it can escalate tensions further.

- **Active Listening:** Listen carefully to their concerns and demands. Show that you understand their perspective, even if you don't agree with it. Active listening can help de-escalate their aggressive stance and demonstrate that you are taking their views seriously.

- **Set Boundaries:** Establish clear boundaries for respectful communication and behavior during the negotiation. Politely but firmly address any unacceptable conduct and request a more constructive approach.

- **Re frame the Conversation:** Redirect the focus of the negotiation from a competitive mindset to a problem-solving orientation. Emphasize the common interests and the potential for mutually beneficial outcomes.

- **Stay Focused on Interests:** Avoid personal attacks or emotional responses. Instead, concentrate on discussing the substantive issues and the interests of both parties.

- **Stay Prepared:** Anticipate aggressive tactics and come prepared with counter arguments and evidence to support your positions. Be ready to defend your points calmly and confidently.

- **Use Objective Criteria:** Rely on objective standards and data to back up your proposals. This approach can neutralize emotional arguments and steer the negotiation towards a more rational path.

- **Take Breaks When Needed:** If emotions are running high, suggest taking a short break to cool off and regroup. Use this time to reassess your strategy and return to the negotiation with a clear mind.

- **Collaborative Language:** Frame your proposals using language that emphasizes cooperation and mutual gain. Show that you are seeking win-win outcomes rather than a zero-sum competition.

- **Involve a Third Party:** If necessary, consider involving a neutral third party or mediator to facilitate the negotiation. Their presence can help maintain civility and ensure a fair process.

- **Explore the Aggressor's Interests:** Try to understand the underlying motivations behind their aggressive behavior. Identifying their needs and concerns may help you find common ground.
- **Be Patient:** Dealing with aggressive negotiators may take time. Stay patient and persistent in your efforts to find constructive solutions.

The key is to respond to aggression with assertiveness, professionalism, and a focus on achieving positive outcomes. By remaining calm, prepared, and collaborative, you can handle aggressive negotiators effectively while still working towards a mutually beneficial agreement.

Strategies for Overcoming Deadlocks and Impasses

Overcoming deadlocks and impasses in negotiations requires a combination of creativity, flexibility, and effective communication. When faced with a stalemate, one of the first steps is to take a break to allow both parties to gain clarity and approach the negotiation with a fresh perspective. Digging deeper to identify the underlying interests and motivations behind each party's positions is crucial.

By understanding the root causes of the deadlock, negotiators can explore multiple options and propose creative solutions that address the parties' core concerns. Emphasizing areas of agreement and shared interests can foster collaboration and help break down barriers. A willingness to trade concessions on less critical issues in exchange for gains on more significant matters can create a balanced give-and-take approach to move the negotiation forward. Utilizing objective criteria and introducing data to evaluate potential solutions adds objectivity to the process. If necessary, involving a neutral third party or mediator can bring a fresh perspective and facilitate constructive communication between the parties. By reframing the issues and focusing on mutual gains, negotiators can shift from a win-lose mentality to a win-win mindset, fostering a cooperative negotiation environment.

Open and transparent communication about needs and concerns builds trust and encourages a more productive negotiation. Considering external factors and evaluating the Best Alternative to a Negotiated Agreement (BATNA) can also contribute to finding flexible and workable solutions. Ultimately, a commitment to problem-solving and a constructive approach are essential for reaching resolutions that satisfy both parties' interests and foster positive, sustainable relationships.

Turning Difficult Negotiations into Opportunities for Growth

Difficult negotiations can be challenging and emotionally taxing, but they also present opportunities for personal and professional growth. Here's how to turn difficult negotiations into valuable learning experiences:

- **Self-Reflection:** Take time to reflect on your emotions and reactions during the negotiation. Identify areas where you might have become defensive or reactive and think about how to improve your emotional intelligence in future negotiations.
- **Identify Learning Points:** Analyze the negotiation process to identify what went well and what could be improved. Assess your strengths and weaknesses as a negotiator and seek to enhance your skills.
- **Seek Feedback:** If possible, ask for feedback from the other party or an impartial observer about your negotiation style. Constructive criticism can help you understand how others perceive your

approach and identify areas for growth.

- **Practice Active Listening:** Improve your active listening skills to better understand the other party's interests and concerns. Practice empathetic listening to build rapport and trust during the negotiation.
- **Manage Emotions:** Develop strategies to manage your emotions effectively during negotiations. Recognize when you are becoming emotional and use techniques like deep breathing or taking a break to regain composure.
- **Embrace Difficulties:** View difficult negotiations as opportunities for growth rather than obstacles. Embracing challenges can help you develop resilience and a positive mindset in high-pressure situations.
- **Learn from Others:** Observe skilled negotiators in action, whether through videos, seminars, or real-life negotiations. Analyze their tactics and strategies and adapt them to your style.
- **Continuous Learning:** Stay updated on negotiation techniques and best practices. Read books, attend workshops, and seek resources to refine your negotiation skills continually.
- **Adaptability:** Recognize that each negotiation is unique, and what works in one situation may not work in another. Be adaptable and open to trying different approaches.
- **Stay Curious:** Cultivate curiosity about the other party's perspective and interests. Ask questions to gain insights and better understand their needs and goals.
- **Celebrate Small Wins:** Acknowledge and celebrate your achievements, no matter how small, during difficult negotiations. Recognizing your progress boosts your confidence and motivates you to keep improving.
- **Focus on Relationships:** Prioritize building positive and constructive relationships with other negotiators. Strong relationships can

lead to smoother negotiations in the future.

- **Keep a Growth Mindset:** Embrace a growth mindset, where challenges are viewed as opportunities for learning and development. Emphasize progress over perfection.

By approaching difficult negotiations with a growth mindset and a commitment to self-improvement, you can turn these challenging situations into valuable learning experiences that enhance your negotiation skills and overall personal growth.

9

Mastering Quick Counteroffers and Compromises

I n fast-paced negotiations, the ability to make quick and strategic counter offers is a valuable skill. In this chapter, we will explore the art of responding to counteroffers effectively, making strategic compromises, and navigating time constraints to secure favorable outcomes efficiently.

Responding to Counteroffers Effectively

Counteroffers are common in negotiations, and the way you respond to them can impact the momentum of the negotiation. We will explore techniques for evaluating counteroffers, understanding the other party's priorities, and formulating persuasive responses that advance your interests while preserving the negotiation's positive trajectory.

Responding to counteroffers effectively is crucial in negotiations to achieve mutually beneficial outcomes. Here are some strategies for handling counteroffers:

- Express appreciation for the counteroffer, regardless of its content, to show respect for the other party's effort.
- Take time to carefully review and analyze the counteroffer's terms in relation to your interests and objectives.
- Revisit your underlying interests and priorities to guide your response and identify potential areas for negotiation.
- Seek clarification if there are any misunderstandings or misinterpretations in the counteroffer.
- Avoid immediately rejecting the counteroffer; explore ways to bridge the gap and find common ground.
- Respond with well-reasoned arguments and data to support your position, avoiding emotional language.
- Emphasize the unique value and benefits of your original proposal.
- Show flexibility by being open to making adjustments to your initial proposal.
- Propose a revised offer that considers the points raised in the counteroffer.
- Keep the communication professional and respectful throughout the negotiation process.
- Reference objective criteria or market standards to support your response.
- Be prepared to walk away if the counteroffer significantly deviates from your interests.
- Maintain open channels of communication to foster understanding and collaboration.
- Seek win-win solutions that benefit both parties.

By responding thoughtfully and strategically to counteroffers, negotiators can navigate the process effectively and work towards achieving mutually satisfactory agreements.

Making Strategic Compromises

Negotiation often involves give-and-take, and making strategic compromises is an essential part of securing win-win outcomes. Making strategic compromises is a vital skill in negotiations, involving finding middle ground while protecting core interests and maximizing overall value. Here are key steps for making strategic compromises:

- **Know your priorities:** Clearly identify must-haves and priorities before negotiating. Understand which issues are essential and where flexibility is possible.
- **Understand the other party's interests:** Analyze their motivations to identify potential compromise areas. Propose solutions that address their needs as well.
- **Explore trade-offs:** Assess potential concessions without sacrificing critical interests. Give up certain aspects to gain concessions in vital areas.
- **Seek mutually beneficial outcomes:** Aim for win-win solutions satisfying both parties' interests, fostering a positive negotiation environment.
- **Use objective criteria:** Rely on fair benchmarks to evaluate compromises, ensuring impartiality.
- **Bundle issues:** Combine multiple issues into packages to create value for both sides, leading to appealing compromises.
- **Make conditional offers:** Propose compromises requiring reciprocal actions, encouraging cooperation.
- **Communicate clearly:** Articulate willingness to compromise while stressing specific objectives and red lines.
- **Build on converging interests:** Focus on shared goals to facilitate collaborative compromises.
- **Consider long-term benefits:** Assess potential compromises'

consequences, weighing short-term concessions against long-term gains.

- **Avoid unilateral concessions:** Aim for balanced compromises, avoiding one-sided concessions without reciprocity.
- **Stay emotionally intelligent:** Manage emotions, maintaining composure under pressure.
- **Be patient:** Recognize that strategic compromises may take time, requiring persistence.

By making strategic compromises, negotiators achieve favorable outcomes, strengthen relationships, and set the stage for successful future collaborations.

Negotiating Under Time Constraints

Time constraints can add pressure to negotiations, necessitating swift decision-making. In this section, we will explore techniques for negotiating effectively under time constraints, maintaining clarity and focus, and preventing rushed decisions that may lead to regrettable outcomes.

Negotiating under time constraints can be challenging, but it's essential to remain focused and adaptable to reach a favorable agreement. Here are some strategies for negotiating effectively when time is limited:

- **Set Priorities:** Identify your most critical objectives and prioritize them. Focus on the key issues that must be addressed to achieve a successful outcome.
- **Prepare in Advance:** Before the negotiation, gather relevant information, anticipate potential challenges, and develop a clear strategy. Being well-prepared will help you make decisions quickly

during the negotiation.

- **Maintain Clear Communication:** Be concise and articulate in your communication. Avoid unnecessary elaboration and get to the point quickly to save time.

- **Be Flexible:** Be prepared to adjust your negotiation approach as needed to accommodate the time constraints. Being flexible and open to creative solutions can expedite the process.

- **Set Time Limits for Each Stage:** Allocate specific time limits for different stages of the negotiation, such as opening statements, proposal discussions, and finalizing the agreement.

- **Focus on Common Ground:** Emphasize areas of agreement and shared interests to find quick resolutions on less contentious issues.

- **Avoid Digressions:** Stay on topic and avoid getting sidetracked by irrelevant or tangential discussions that can waste time.

- **Use Summaries:** Summarize key points periodically to ensure all parties are on the same page and avoid unnecessary repetition.

- **Consider the Other Party's Time Constraints:** Understand that the other party may also be under time pressure. Be respectful of their time limitations to foster cooperation.

- **Be Decisive:** Make timely decisions and avoid unnecessary delays in responding to offers or proposals.

- **Limit Concessions:** Be cautious about making extensive concessions without careful consideration. Make sure each concession aligns with your priorities and interests.

- **Negotiate in Good Faith:** Demonstrate a sincere commitment to finding a resolution despite the time constraints. This can encourage reciprocity and cooperation from the other party.

- **Use Short Breaks Wisely:** If there are moments to pause for reflection or consultation, use short breaks efficiently to regroup and strategize.

Negotiating under time constraints requires efficiency, focus, and adaptability. By setting priorities, preparing well, and staying flexible, negotiators can navigate time-limited negotiations successfully and achieve positive outcomes.

10

Closing the Deal and Ensuring Long-Term Success

C losing the deal is the culmination of your negotiation efforts, but the process doesn't end there. In this chapter, we will explore the crucial steps to finalize negotiations successfully, formalize agreements, and ensure long-term success and satisfaction for all parties involved.

The Importance of Formalizing Agreements

Formalizing agreements is a critical step to ensure that all parties have a clear understanding of the terms and commitments. We will discuss the significance of written agreements, including the necessary components and potential pitfalls to avoid when drafting contracts.

Formalizing agreements in negotiations is crucial due to several key reasons:

- **Clarity and Understanding:** A formal agreement clearly outlines the terms, conditions, and expectations of both parties, reducing ambiguity and misunderstandings.

- **Preventing Disputes:** Written agreements decrease the likelihood of future disputes as parties can refer back to the agreement to resolve disagreements.

- **Legal Protection:** Formal agreements often include legal language and clauses that protect the rights and interests of all parties, making them more enforceable in court.

- **Building Trust:** Formalizing agreements demonstrates professionalism and commitment, fostering trust between the negotiating parties.

- **Facilitating Compliance:** A written agreement encourages all parties to adhere to the agreed-upon terms, ensuring better compliance.

- **Managing Expectations:** Formal agreements specify deliverables, timelines, and responsibilities, managing expectations and reducing risks of unmet expectations.

Formalizing agreements establishes clear expectations, prevents disputes, protects parties' interests, and creates a solid foundation for successful and professional relationships. It provides structure and legal support, ensuring both parties fulfill their commitments and achieve desired outcomes.

Documenting Terms and Clarity

Clear and concise documentation of the negotiated terms is essential to prevent misunderstandings and disputes in the future. We will explore techniques for documenting the agreed-upon terms, addressing potential contingencies, and ensuring that the final agreement aligns with the intentions of both parties.

Strategies for Successful Deal-Closing

The final steps of negotiation require finesse and tact. We will discuss strategies for effectively closing the deal, including summarizing key points, addressing any last-minute concerns, and expressing gratitude for the collaborative effort.

Successfully closing a deal in negotiations requires a combination of strategic planning and effective communication. Here are key strategies for achieving deal-closing success:

- **Maintain Rapport:** Establish a strong relationship with the other party to foster trust and cooperation.
- **Understand Motivations:** Gain deep insights into the other party's needs and tailor your proposal accordingly.
- **Focus on Value:** Emphasize the benefits of the deal and how it aligns with their goals.
- **Address Concerns Proactively:** Anticipate objections and provide well-prepared responses.
- **Create a Win-Win Outcome:** Seek mutually beneficial solutions for both parties.
- Present a Strong Case: Use compelling data and evidence to support your proposal.
- **Be Flexible:** Show willingness to make reasonable adjustments to accommodate their needs.
- **Summarize Key Points:** Recap the agreement to ensure clarity and alignment.
- **Set a Deadline:** Establish a reasonable timeframe to encourage timely decisions.
- **Leverage Scarcity and Urgency:** Highlight time-sensitive benefits or limited availability.

- **Overcome Obstacles Together:** Collaborate to find solutions to challenges.
- **Follow Up and Confirm:** Formalize the agreement in writing for clarity.
- **Celebrate Success:** Acknowledge the achievement and express gratitude.

By implementing these strategies, negotiators can enhance their chances of closing deals successfully and achieving positive outcomes that benefit all parties involved.

Maintaining Relationships After the Negotiation

Long-lasting relationships are crucial for future opportunities and continued success. We will explore techniques for maintaining positive relationships after the negotiation, including follow-up communications, regular check-ins, and recognizing and appreciating the contributions of all parties involved.

11

Post-Negotiation Strategies

Analyzing the Results of Negotiation

After the negotiation process concludes, it is essential to evaluate the results and outcomes. This chapter will guide you through the post-negotiation analysis, where you'll learn how to assess whether the agreement meets your objectives and whether you achieved a favorable outcome. We will explore techniques to measure success, review key performance indicators, and identify areas for improvement.

Evaluating Your Performance and Learning from Experience

Self-assessment is a crucial aspect of becoming a proficient negotiator. In this section, we will delve into the importance of evaluating your performance in negotiations. By reflecting on your strengths and weaknesses, you can identify areas for growth and development. Analyzing the results of a negotiation is crucial for assessing its effectiveness and understanding how well the goals were achieved.

Here are some key steps and considerations for analyzing the results of a negotiation:

- **Review the Initial Objectives:** Start by revisiting the original objectives and goals set before the negotiation. Compare these objectives with the final outcomes to determine if they were met, partially met, or not met at all.

- **Assess the Outcomes:** Evaluate the specific outcomes of the negotiation, such as agreements reached, concessions made, and any compromises involved. Consider both the tangible and intangible gains and losses resulting from the negotiation.

- **Quantitative Analysis:** If possible, quantify the results in measurable terms. For example, if the negotiation involved a financial deal, analyze the cost savings, revenue gains, or profitability implications. Quantitative analysis helps provide a clear picture of the negotiation's impact.

- **Qualitative Analysis:** In addition to quantitative aspects, consider the qualitative factors, such as improved relationships, strengthened partnerships, or enhanced reputations resulting from the negotiation.

- **Compare with Alternatives:** Analyze the negotiated outcomes by comparing them with the alternatives. Consider the best alternative to a negotiated agreement (BATNA) and the worst alternative to a negotiated agreement (WATNA) to understand how well the negotiation performed compared to the available alternatives.

- **Determine Success Criteria:** Define the criteria for success before analyzing the results. Success may not always mean getting everything desired; it might involve finding a fair compromise or achieving essential objectives while maintaining relationships.

- **Consider Long-Term Implications:** Assess the potential long-term consequences of the negotiated agreement. Will it lead to sustainable partnerships and positive future interactions, or are there any potential pitfalls to watch out for?

- **Identify Lessons Learned:** Reflect on the negotiation process and identify areas of improvement. Assess what went well and what could have been done differently to achieve better results in future negotiations.

- **Seek Feedback:** If possible, gather feedback from all parties involved in the negotiation. Understanding how they perceive the results can provide valuable insights into the effectiveness of the negotiation process and outcomes.

- **Reflect on Communication and Strategy:** Analyze how well communication was handled during the negotiation and whether the chosen negotiation strategies were effective. This reflection can inform future negotiation approaches.

- **Adjust Future Approaches:** Based on the analysis, make adjustments to future negotiation strategies and tactics. Continuous improvement is essential in the art of negotiation.

By thoroughly analyzing the results of a negotiation, you can learn from the experience and become more effective in future negotiations. It allows you to build upon strengths and address weaknesses to achieve better outcomes in your negotiation endeavors.

Building Long-Term Relationships

Successful negotiators understand the significance of building and maintaining long-term relationships. This chapter will explore how to foster positive relationships with your negotiation counterparts, even after the deal is closed. Building long-term relationships is essential in both personal and professional settings. Long-lasting relationships can lead to trust, mutual support, and various opportunities.

Here are some key principles and strategies for fostering and maintaining strong, long-term relationships:

- **Communication:** Open and honest communication is the foundation of any successful relationship. Actively listen to others, express your thoughts and feelings clearly, and encourage open dialogue. Good communication helps in resolving conflicts and prevents misunderstandings.
- **Trust:** Trust is the cornerstone of long-term relationships. Be reliable, consistent, and keep your promises. Avoid actions that can break trust, and if trust is broken, work on rebuilding it through transparency and accountability.
- **Empathy and Understanding:** Show empathy towards others by putting yourself in their shoes and understanding their perspectives. Being supportive and understanding helps create a deeper connection and fosters a sense of mutual respect.
- **Respect:** Treat others with respect, regardless of their position or background. Respect their opinions, boundaries, and values. Respecting others fosters a positive environment and encourages reciprocal respect.
- **Shared Values and Goals:** Establish common ground with others by identifying shared values and goals. Having similar aspirations strengthens the bond and makes it easier to collaborate on projects and initiatives.
- **Be Supportive:** Offer support and encouragement to others in their endeavors. Celebrate their successes and provide a helping hand during challenging times. Supportive relationships build a sense of community and loyalty.
- **Give and Take:** Strive for a balanced exchange in the relationship. Be willing to give and contribute to others' needs while also being open to receiving support when you require it.

- **Resolve Conflicts Gracefully:** Conflicts are natural in any relationship. When disagreements arise, address them calmly and constructively. Focus on finding solutions rather than placing blame.
- **Demonstrate Appreciation:** Express gratitude and appreciation for the people in your life. Acknowledging their contributions and efforts reinforces positive behaviors and strengthens the bond.
- **Stay Connected:** Regularly engage with the individuals in your network. Whether it's through social gatherings, meetings, or virtual communication, staying connected helps maintain the relationship.
- **Adapt and Grow Together:** People change and evolve over time. Be open to embracing change and growing together in your relationships. Embrace new experiences and challenges as opportunities for personal and relational growth.
- **Give Without Expecting Immediate Returns:** Building strong relationships requires patience and a genuine willingness to invest in others without expecting instant rewards. Understand that building trust and rapport takes time and consistent effort.
- **Apologize and Forgive:** When you make mistakes, apologize sincerely. Similarly, be willing to forgive others for their shortcomings. Learning to forgive and seek forgiveness helps maintain harmony in relationships.

Building long-term relationships is an ongoing process that requires active participation, understanding, and commitment from all parties involved. By following these principles and strategies, you can foster meaningful connections and cultivate a network of valuable and enduring relationships.

12

Negotiating with Yourself

Setting Personal Goals and Priorities

Before entering any negotiation, it's vital to know yourself and your objectives. In this chapter, you will learn the importance of setting clear personal goals and priorities. By aligning your internal values with your negotiation goals, you can maintain focus and make informed decisions that align with your broader aspirations.

Setting personal goals and priorities is essential for personal growth, fulfillment, and achieving a sense of purpose. Here's a step-by-step guide to help you effectively set personal goals and priorities:

- **Self-Reflection:** Take some time to reflect on your values, passions, strengths, and areas for improvement. Consider what brings you joy, what you want to achieve in life, and what matters most to you. This self-awareness will help you align your goals with your true desires.
- **Define Your Long-Term Vision:** Envision where you want to

be in the future. Create a clear and compelling vision of what you want your life to look like in the next five, ten, or twenty years. Your long-term vision will serve as a guiding light for setting your goals and priorities.

- **Set SMART Goals:** Create specific, measurable, achievable, relevant, and time-bound (SMART) goals. Be clear about what you want to accomplish, how you will measure success, and set a deadline for achieving each goal.

- **Prioritize Your Goals:** It's crucial to prioritize your goals based on their importance and urgency. Identify the most critical objectives that align with your long-term vision and values. Focus on a few key goals rather than spreading yourself too thin.

- **Break Down Larger Goals:** Divide big, long-term goals into smaller, manageable milestones. This approach will make the goals less overwhelming and enable you to track your progress more effectively.

- **Develop an Action Plan:** Create a detailed action plan for each goal. Outline the steps you need to take, the resources required, and the timeline for completion. Having a clear plan will keep you organized and motivated.

- **Consider Potential Obstacles:** Anticipate potential challenges and obstacles that may hinder your progress. Identify ways to overcome them and stay resilient in the face of setbacks.

- **Be Flexible:** Life is unpredictable, and circumstances may change. Be willing to adapt your goals and priorities as needed. Stay open to new opportunities and be ready to adjust your course when necessary.

- **Review and Reassess Regularly:** Set aside time regularly (e.g., monthly or quarterly) to review your progress. Celebrate your achievements, assess any setbacks, and adjust your goals and priorities if required. Regular reviews keep you on track and motivated.

- **Focus on Self-Care:** Taking care of yourself is essential for goal achievement. Prioritize self-care activities such as exercise, adequate sleep, healthy eating, and spending time with loved ones. A balanced and healthy lifestyle will help you stay energized and focused.

- **Stay Accountable:** Share your goals with a trusted friend, family member, or mentor who can support and hold you accountable. Having someone to discuss your progress with can keep you motivated and responsible.

- **Celebrate Milestones:** Acknowledge and celebrate your achievements along the way. Rewarding yourself for reaching milestones will boost your morale and reinforce positive behaviors.

Setting personal goals and priorities is an ongoing process. As you accomplish your goals, new aspirations and ambitions may arise, leading you to redefine your priorities. Stay committed to personal growth and continuously refine your goals to lead a fulfilling and purpose-driven life.

Overcoming Self-Limiting Beliefs

Self-doubt and limiting beliefs can hinder your negotiation performance. In this section, we'll explore various common self-limiting beliefs and how to overcome them. By cultivating a positive and growth-oriented mindset, you can bolster your confidence and navigate negotiations with a renewed sense of empowerment.

Overcoming self-limiting beliefs is crucial for personal growth and achieving success. Self-limiting beliefs are negative thoughts or assumptions we hold about ourselves that hinder our progress and prevent us from reaching our full potential. Here are some steps to help you overcome self-limiting beliefs:

- **Identify Your Self-Limiting Beliefs**: Become aware of negative thoughts and assumptions you hold about yourself.
- **Challenge Your Beliefs:** Question the validity of these beliefs and look for evidence to support or refute them.
- **Replace with Positive Affirmations:** Replace self-limiting beliefs with positive statements about yourself.
- **Seek Support:** Talk to others about your beliefs to gain perspective and encouragement.
- **Set Realistic Goals:** Break down larger goals into achievable steps to build confidence.
- **Celebrate Your Achievements:** Acknowledge and celebrate even small successes.
- Reframe Failures: View failures as opportunities for growth and learning.
- **Visualize Success:** Imagine yourself succeeding and achieving your goals.
- Surround Yourself with Positive Influences: Be around supportive and encouraging people.
- **Take Action:** Step outside your comfort zone and take action toward your goals.
- practice Self-Compassion: Treat yourself with kindness and understanding.
- **Monitor Progress:** Keep track of your achievements and progress.

By following these steps, you can overcome self-limiting beliefs and unlock your true potential.

Developing a Strong Negotiating Mindset

A strong negotiating mindset is a key differentiator between average negotiators and exceptional ones. Developing a strong negotiating mindset is essential for achieving successful outcomes in any negotiation. A positive and strategic mindset can help you approach negotiations with confidence, flexibility, and a focus on mutual gain.

Here are some tips to develop a strong negotiating mindset:

- **Be Prepared:** Thoroughly research the negotiation topic, understand the other party's interests, and anticipate potential challenges. Preparedness instills confidence and allows you to make well-informed decisions during the negotiation.
- **Stay Calm and Confident:** Keep your emotions in check during the negotiation process. A calm and composed demeanor demonstrates confidence and helps you think clearly under pressure.
- **Listen Actively:** Effective negotiation involves active listening. Pay attention to the other party's needs, concerns, and perspectives. Listening helps you identify common ground and areas for compromise.
- **Be Flexible and Adaptable:** Negotiations often involve unexpected twists. Be willing to adapt your strategies and explore alternative solutions to reach a satisfactory agreement.
- **Know Your Limits:** Define your objectives and boundaries before entering the negotiation. Knowing your limits allows you to make principled concessions without compromising your core interests.
- **Communicate Clearly:** Articulate your thoughts, proposals, and concerns clearly and succinctly. Clarity in communication minimizes misunderstandings and helps build rapport.
- **Maintain a Positive Attitude:** A positive attitude can create a conducive atmosphere for constructive dialogue. Avoid aggressive or hostile behavior, as it can hinder productive negotiations.

- **Be Patient:** Negotiations can take time, especially when dealing with complex issues. Stay patient and avoid rushing the process, as impatience can lead to unfavorable outcomes.

- **Recognize Non-Verbal Cues:** Pay attention to non-verbal cues from the other party, such as body language and tone of voice. Understanding these cues can provide valuable insights into their position and emotions.

- **Learn from Experience:** Reflect on past negotiations, identify strengths, and areas for improvement. Learning from experience allows you to refine your approach and become a more effective negotiator over time.

- **Stay Ethical:** Maintain your integrity throughout the negotiation process. Honesty and ethical behavior build trust, which is crucial for successful negotiations and long-term relationships.

- **Handle Deadlocks Constructively:** Deadlocks and disagreements are common in negotiations. Approach them as opportunities for creative problem-solving rather than as roadblocks.

- **Celebrate Successes:** Acknowledge and celebrate successful negotiations, whether big or small. Celebrating achievements reinforces positive behavior and boosts confidence for future negotiations.

Developing a strong negotiating mindset is a continuous journey of learning and self-improvement. By adopting these strategies and maintaining a positive and constructive approach, you can enhance your negotiation skills and achieve better outcomes in your personal and professional life.

13

Conclusion

"The Quick Negotiator" has been a journey into the world of negotiation, equipping you with a diverse array of practical techniques to thrive in various negotiation scenarios. From understanding the foundations of negotiation and mastering active listening and communication to leveraging empathy and emotional intelligence, you have gained valuable insights into the art of persuasion and deal making. Throughout this book, we emphasized the significance of creating win-win solutions, navigating difficult negotiation situations, and mastering quick counteroffers and compromises. You have learned to embrace preparation as the key to negotiation success, laying a strong foundation for swift and efficient negotiations.

Remember that negotiation is not just about achieving personal victories; it is about creating collaborative and mutually beneficial outcomes. By approaching negotiation with empathy, integrity, and respect, you can foster long-term relationships and achieve sustainable success in your endeavors.

CONCLUSION

As you continue your journey as a quick negotiator, practice and refine the techniques presented in this book. Adapt them to your unique style, and remember that negotiation is a continuous learning process. Embrace challenges as opportunities for growth and improvement. The art of negotiation is dynamic, and there will always be new scenarios and contexts to explore. Embrace each negotiation as a chance to refine your skills and create positive, lasting outcomes. As you apply the knowledge gained from "The Quick Negotiator," I have no doubt that you will continue to excel in the art of persuasion and deal making.

Good luck on your negotiation adventures, and may your ability to negotiate swiftly and effectively lead you to unparalleled success in all your endeavors. If you found this book helpful, take a moment to leave a positive review on Amazon or any reading or listening platform.